Kirklees

CULTURAL SERVICES

Cultural Services Headquarters
Red Doles Lane
Huddersfield
HD2 1YF

D1381143

SCISSOR SISTERS

Published 2005

© International Music Publications Ltd.
Griffin House 161 Hammersmith Road, London W6 8BS England

Arranged and engraved by Artemis Music Ltd. (www.artemismusic.com)

LAURA

Words and Music by Scott Hoffman and Jason Sellards

don't you give me your.

This - 'll be the last time___

TAKE YOUR MAMA

Words and Music by Scott Hoffman and Jason Sellards

1. When you grow up   liv - in' like a good boy
2. It's a strug - gle,   liv - in' like a good boy

ought-a   and your ma - ma   takes_ a shine to her best   son,   some thing
ought-a   in the sum - mer,   watch in' all the girls pass   by.   When your

COMFORTABLY NUMB

Words and Music by George Roger Waters and David Gilmour

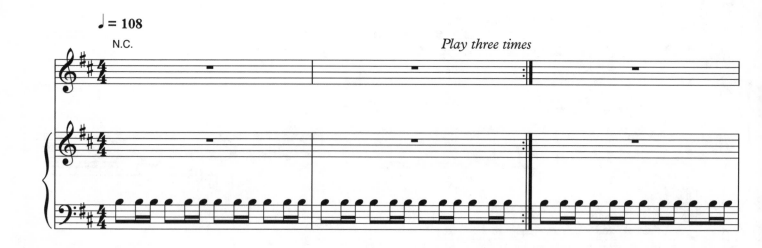

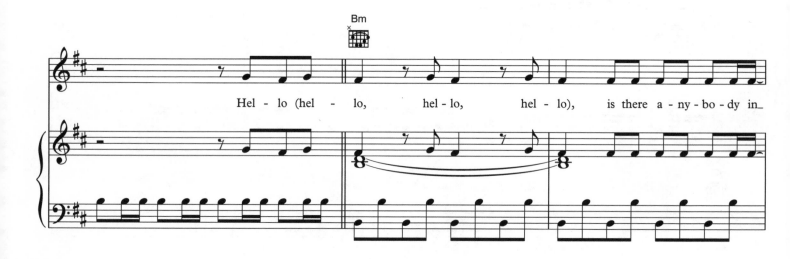

Got-ta keep it go-ing through the show, come on,___ it's time to go.

I, I, have be - come com - fort-ably numb.___

MARY

Words and Music by Scott Hoffman and Jason Sellards

1. I love the tone that's in your laugh, gasp-ing for an ex-
2. I've had it ea-sy now, you see. When I'm down you're al-

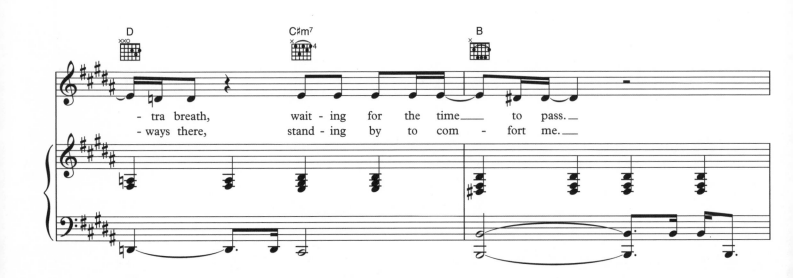

- tra breath, wait-ing for the time to pass.
- ways there, stand-ing by to com-fort me.

TITS ON THE RADIO

Words and Music by Scott Hoffman, Jason Sellards and Ana Lynch

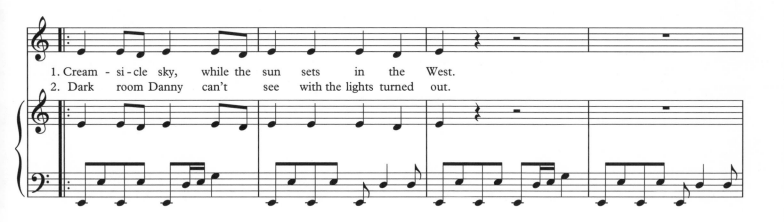

1. Cream - si - cle sky, while the sun sets in the West.
2. Dark room Danny can't see with the lights turned out.

Where are the queers on the piers? Heard they gave it their best.
Black - haired tranny counts sheep with her bed turned down. But the

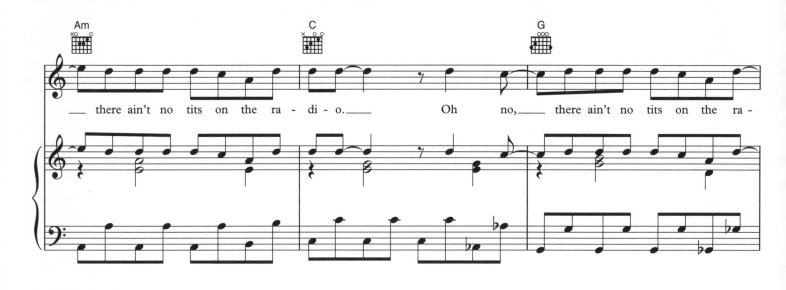

there ain't no tits on the ra - di - o.___ Oh no,___ there ain't no tits on the ra-

1.

- di - o,___ no, no.___

2.

- di - o,___ no, no.___ There ain't no tits on the ra - di - o.___ Oh no,_

'Cause you can't see tits on the ra - di - o. I'll

LOVERS IN THE BACKSEAT

Words and Music by Scott Hoffman and Jason Sellards

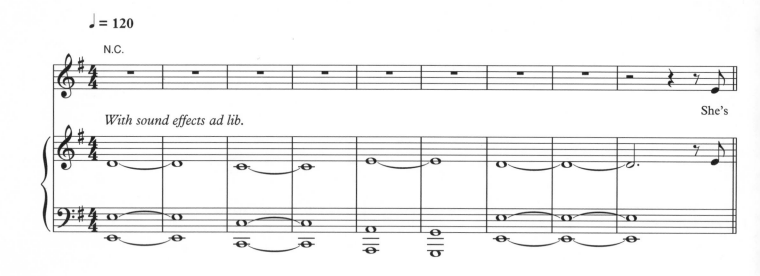

FILTHY/GORGEOUS

Words and Music by Scott Hoffman, Jason Sellards and Ana Lynch

Spoken: Oh you're so gorgeous.

C5

1, 2.

3.

When you're

MUSIC IS THE VICTIM

Words and Music by Scott Hoffman, Jason Sellards and Derek Gruen

BETTER LUCK

Words and Music by Scott Hoffman, Jason Sellards and Derek Gruen

love, one that car - ries on. Bet - ter luck next time.__ Guess I've on - ly one re -

-gret, that I did - n't get to know you bet - ter than I did.

IT CAN'T COME QUICKLY ENOUGH

Words and Music by Scott Hoffman and Jason Sellards

RETURN TO OZ

Words and Music by Scott Hoffman and Jason Sellards

$\quad$ = 72

1.Once there was a man_ who had a lit-tle too much time on his hands.
2. *See block lyrics*

_ He ne-ver stopped to think_ that he was get-ting_ old- er. When his

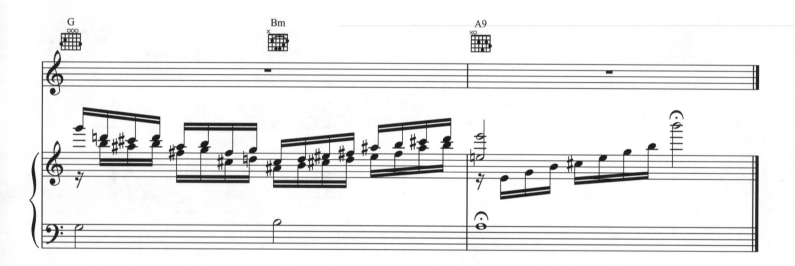

Verse 2:
It's three o'clock in the morning.
You get a phone call from the queen
With a hundred heads.
She says they're all dead.
She tried the last one on.
It couldn't speak, fell off.
And now she just wanders the halls
Thinking nothing, nothing at all.

She says is this the return to Oz?
The grass is dead, the gold is brown
And the sky has claws.
There's a wind-up man
Walking round and round.
What once was Emerald City's
Now a crystal town.